MW01097859

WWW.BENDOCKERY.COM

10 CHRISTMAS DUETS VOL. 4

CONTENTS

ARRANGEMENTS BY B. C. DOCKERY ©2022

Angels From the Realm of Glory

Henry Smart
B. C. Dockery

Coventry Carol

Traditional
B. C. Dockery

Gesu Bambino

Pietro Yon
B. C. Dockery

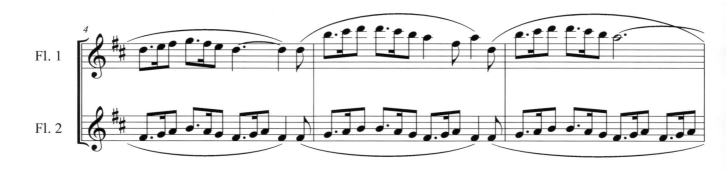

Arr. ©2022

Good Christian Men, Rejoice!

Traditional German
B. C. Dockery

Arr. ©2022

Lo, How a Rose E'er Blooming

Traditional
B. C. Dockery

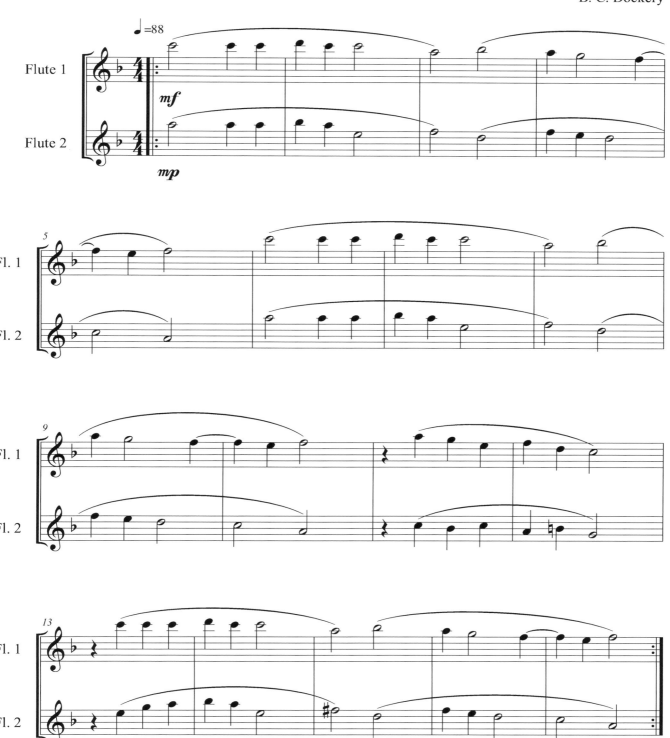

O Christmas Tree

O Tannenbaum

Traditional German
B. C. Dockery

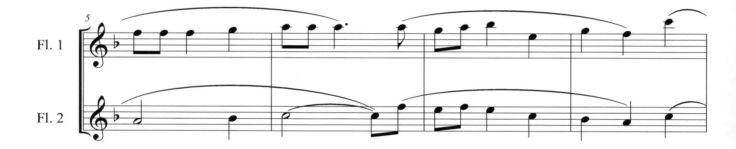

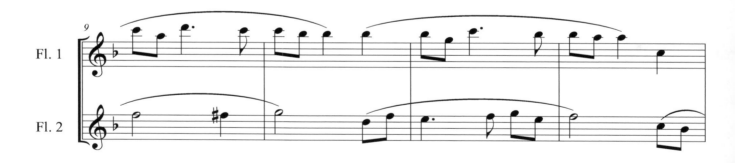

Arr. ©2022

The Holly and the Ivy

Traditional English
B. C. Dockery

Up on the Housetop

Benjamin Hanby
B. C. Dockery

Here We Come A-Caroling

Wassail Song

Traditional English
B. C. Dockery

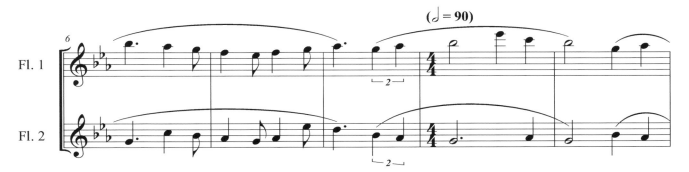

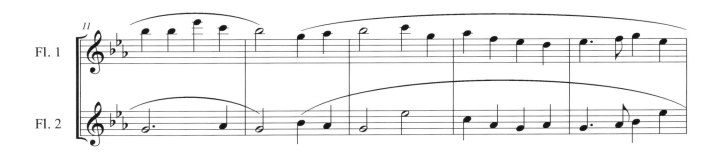

Arr. ©2022

While Shepherds Watched Their Flock

Nahum Tate

B. C. Dockery

Angels From the Realm of Glory

Flute 1

Henry Smart
B. C. Dockery

Angels From the Realm of Glory

Flute 2

Henry Smart
B. C. Dockery

Arr. ©2022

Coventry Carol

Flute 1

Traditional
B. C. Dockery

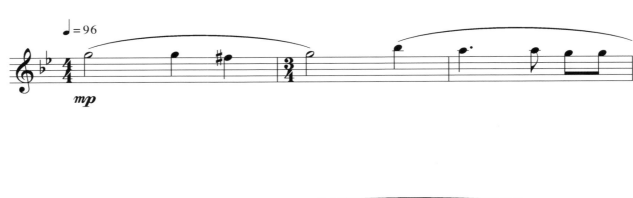

Arr. ©2022

Coventry Carol

Flute 2

Traditional
B. C. Dockery

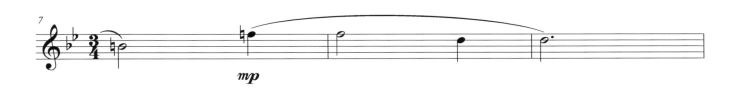

Gesu Bambino

Flute 1

Pietro Yon
B. C. Dockery

Gesu Bambino

Flute 2

Pietro Yon
B. C. Dockery

Good Christian Men, Rejoice!

Flute 1

Traditional German
B. C. Dockery

Good Christian Men, Rejoice!

Flute 2

Traditional German
B. C. Dockery

Lo, How a Rose E'er Blooming

Flute 1

Traditional
B. C. Dockery

Arr. ©2022

Lo, How a Rose E'er Blooming

Flute 2

Traditional
B. C. Dockery

Arr. ©2022

O Christmas Tree
O Tannenbaum

Flute 1

Traditional German
B. C. Dockery

O Christmas Tree
O Tannenbaum

Flute 2

Traditional German
B. C. Dockery

Arr. ©2022

The Holly and the Ivy

Flute 1

Traditional English
B. C. Dockery

The Holly and the Ivy

Flute 2

Traditional English
B. C. Dockery

Arr. ©2022

Up on the Housetop

Flute 1

Benjamin Hanby
B. C. Dockery

Arr. ©2022

Up on the Housetop

Flute 2

Benjamin Hanby
B. C. Dockery

Here We Come A-Caroling

Wassail Song

Flute 1

Traditional English
B. C. Dockery

Arr. ©2022

Here We Come A-Caroling

Flute 2

Wassail Song

Traditional English
B. C. Dockery

Arr. ©2022

2

While Shepherds Watched Their Flock

Flute 1

Nahum Tate
B. C. Dockery

Arr. ©2022

While Shepherds Watched Their Flock

Flute 2

Nahum Tate

B. C. Dockery

Made in the USA
Las Vegas, NV
25 November 2023

81508793R00020